It's the Most Wonderful Time of the Year

by
Judy Condon

©2013 Marsh Homestead Country Antiques, LLC

Library of Congress Cataloging-in-Publications Data
It's the Most Wonderful Time of the Year by Judy Condon
ISBN 978-0-9847028-7-9

Oceanic Graphic Printing, Inc.
105 Main Street
Hackensack, NJ 07601

Printed in China

Layout and Design by Pat Lucas,
    lucasketch_design@yahoo.com
Edited by Trent Michaels

Table of Contents

About the Author

Judy Condon is a native New Englander, which is evident in her decorating style and the type of antiques she collects and sells. Her real passion is 19thC authentic dry red or blue painted pieces. While Judy enjoyed a professional career as a teacher, Principal, and Superintendent of Schools in Connecticut, Judy's weekends were spent at her antique shop, *Marsh Homestead Country Antiques*, located in Litchfield, Connecticut.

When her husband, Jeff, was relocated to Virginia, Judy accepted an early retirement from education and concentrated her energy and passion for antiques into a fulltime business. Judy maintains a website, *www.marshhomesteadantiques. com* and has been a Power Seller on eBay® for 13 years under the name "superct".

Judy and her husband Jeff recently returned to their roots in New England and have completed renovating a 19thC cape in Massachusetts. The house was featured in her early 2012 book *Back Home – Simply Country* which included many before and after pictures. Judy has five children and five grandchildren and enjoys reading, golf, bridge, tennis, and volunteering in the educational system in St Maarten. Judy does her best to provide teaching materials and children's books to the schools in St. Maarten with the hope of helping establish classroom libraries.

Judy's first 25 books in the "simply country" series, *Country on a Shoestring, Of Hearth and Home – Simply Country, A Simpler Time, Country Decorating for All Seasons, As Time Goes By, Country at Heart, Welcome Home – Simply Country, Home Again – Simply Country, The Warmth of Home, The Country Home, Simple Greens – Simply Country, The Country Life, Simply Country Gardens, Simply Country Gardens, The Spirit of Country, The Joy of Country, Holidays at a Country Home, A Touch of Country, Back Home-Simply Country, Just Country Gardens, The Place We Call Home, Autumn Harvest, Stockings Were Hung, Make It Country, Through the Garden Gate* and *The Way It Was* have been instant hits and some are in their second printing. Judy continues to pursue additional homes and gardens and is working on four books for publication in 2014. Her books are available on her Website – *www.marshhomesteadantiques.com*, *Amazon.com*, through her email marshhomestead@comcast.net, or by phone at 877-381-6682.

Introduction

The tree is up, the house is filled with greens and berries, the cookies are baked and the holiday music is playing. With my shopping complete, I set aside a quiet afternoon in front of the fire and began the process of writing my Christmas cards. Once a year I pull from the desk drawer my address book which I have kept for over 50 years; so many pages marked with a large 'X' over the names of those who were deceased or with whom I had lost contact. It was time to transfer into a new book only those names who would receive a card.

Mabel Allen no longer lives at 111 Elm Street, for she had passed away 38 years ago, yet I still hear Auntie Mabel's voice whispering, "Nightly night. Sleep tight. Don't let the bed bugs bite," as she tucked me into bed as a small child. Eldridge Price, gone 40 years now, introduced me to the movies as a young child on Saturday night where, for 35 cents, we saw a double feature, often an Abbott & Costello in black and white AND a newsreel!

My great Aunt Florence, still fresh in my mind's eye, stands next to the piano on Christmas Day singing 'O Holy Night'. Sally Johnson lived in the apartment next door 39 years ago when I first married and we shared the same challenges as new mothers. I found childhood friends with whom I had idled away endless hours during summer vacations and a college roommate who, like me, was now a grandmother. I remembered Aunt Connie who took my siblings and me for an annual trip to New York City in December for a full day of activities. While I relish the anticipation of what the future will bring, I thoroughly enjoyed sharing time with the past.

After all, do we not try to replicate the aura and traditions of our Christmases past when we decorate for the season? I turned the page to the names beginning with the letter 'M' to find a new entry – a new friend. The present.

My mother began a family tradition 45 years ago by creating handmade pewter ornaments that reflected a special event from the previous year. One summer our family traveled to the White Mountains in New Hampshire, and that Christmas we received a pewter ornament of a moose. Each January, the girls in the family traveled to a spa for a weekend with my mom. That year we received an ornament depicting the spa's logo, a Fat Bird. I now have enough pewter ornaments

to fill a small tree, and each year as I carefully hang them, I reflect on each ornament's special memory. My mother taught my niece Jane to work with pewter and Jane now carries on the family tradition.

When the last card was addressed, I closed my new address book to which I had carefully transferred all the names from my other three books. Unable to eliminate anyone, I placed the book back in my desk drawer, looking forward to next year when I can again reflect at Christmastime on those special people who touched my life. I hope you can take a minute out of your hectic holiday schedule to reflect on those holidays of the past and enjoy the memories of those we each hold in our hearts because truly It's The Most Wonderful Time of the Year.

Chapter 1

❧ ✿ ☙

Jim and Gerry Hendrickson

Jim and Gerry Hendrickson live in Sumerduck, Virginia, located approximately 10 miles outside of Fredericksburg. Gerry became a customer of my shop and we struck up an acquaintance through a common passion for early paint and country pieces.

Jim, a native of Illinois, is retired from the Marine Corps Exchange Service and keeps busy restoring classic Chevrolet automobiles. Gerry has worked for over 30 years as an administrative assistant for a company in Chantilly. More than once she mentioned how an errand related to an antique caused her to race out during lunchtime or at the end of the day.

The door with early red paint was stored behind the shed in the backyard until Gerry came up with the brilliant idea to place it on the back porch behind an early blue painted potting table that Gerry received from her mother; I love the colors together.

Gerry and Jim built their home 12 years ago and modified the plans to accommodate some of their larger antique pieces.

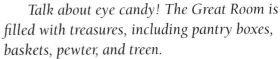

Talk about eye candy! The Great Room is filled with treasures, including pantry boxes, baskets, pewter, and treen.

The buttery table in early red paint is from Sandy Hart in New Oxford, Pennsylvania; Gerry fills it seasonally with vegetables or fruits. Here she displays red and white potatoes, onions, and carrots. A colander on the floor holds white beans.

Gerry has placed a paper mache Santa face over a large Bible Box lid on the wall beside the blanket crane.

An early tavern table with red base holds fruit and assorted greens in vintage dough bowls.

An open wall cupboard holds assorted pieces of Bennington pottery. A chest beneath it features original red paint and holds a set of yellowware plates.

The train belonged to Jim as a boy; it stands beneath an early wagon purchased years ago at a yard sale. Gerry couldn't remember if she paid 25 cents or $1.00.

A board used for chipping herbs or kneading dough was purchased from Lynn Oppenheimer, whose home was featured in an earlier book.

Jim and Gerry purchased the buttery shelves from Ginny Curry Antiques in Ohio. Gerry particularly likes the spoon rack on the second shelf from the top. An apple peeler on the second shelf from the bottom, right hand side, is a three-legged Shaker piece and constructed without nails.

The case and face are original to the tall standing clock, although the workings have been replaced. Gerry has never regretted its purchase and enjoys its primitive look and the fact that it tilts a bit to the left.

An old hay ladder leans in the corner of the foyer. I love the blue hanging cupboard. An apothecary against the opposite wall contains a number of drawers with pencil written notations inside, such as 'whole nutmeg 3 cents/lb'.

The décor in a small powder room is built around the vintage wall print of a little girl with a blue ribbon in her hair.

A vintage coverlet remnant in the Lee's Surrender pattern is displayed on the dining room table. Gerry often antiques with friend Linda Beach and they purchased the coverlet for $75 and then split the good pieces between them.

An open stepback holds a collection of spatter ware and a folksy handmade Santa figure.

Gerry found the bucket bench, seen left, at Ivy Hill Antiques in Pennsylvania. Again, she was drawn to it because of the unique spoon rack on the back. Gerry uses the clusters of red berries called Nandina berries in many of her decorations, as they last for months and the color remains vibrant.

Gerry first saw the southern biscuit table, seen left, at a show and passed it up. It spoke to her all night and the next day she drove all the way to North Carolina. She was surprised when she saw the table in the daylight as it didn't seem to look quite as nice as it had at the show. Over the next year, with elbow grease and determination, Gerry dry scraped and used steel wool on it; she is now quite pleased with the results. After the dough is kneaded and ready to rise, it is placed in the center hole. The top lifts down to keep the dough warm. A bin on either side of the hole holds flour and meal.

The island in Gerry's kitchen is an old store counter found in Illinois. Gerry raced home from work to instruct the carpenter how she wanted the counter adapted with barn wood to fit her kitchen décor.

Gerry scraped the bench in the kitchen that she said had about 50 shades of paint. It has a zinc top and zinc across the back indicating it may have been used as a cutting table.

The hollowed out log on legs that Gerry has filled with greens and pine cones features a hole in the bottom; it may have been an early primitive sink.

Gerry has filled a cupboard in the kitchen eating area with Rowe pottery. The large ornaments on top are painted to look like salt-glazed pottery.

A laundry room is country decorated with all the necessities for wash day.

Gerry told about another frantic ride home from the office to catch the contractor who was about to modify a wall to accommodate the large cupboard from Illinois. The cupboard was an unexpected acquisition from Jim's family that Gerry uses to display quilts and coverlets. A small wall hanging cupboard with original red wash holds a collection of miniature vintage paper houses.

A corner of the TV room holds a beautiful painted apothecary and vintage clothing. A half-tree allows extra space in the room and is filled with cotton batting ornaments.

The pie safe with tin panels conceals a television. Gerry bought the 19thC chimney cupboard with green paint from Marsh Homestead Antiques! Hmmm . . . what was I thinking?

Gerry has hung small stockings and mittens on the fireplace board at one end of the room. The portrait depicts Robert E. Lee, an original work by the late Joe Umble. The picture also shows a group of marching Civil War soldiers surrounded by smoke.

Gerry and Jim use the large sunroom to entertain, an ideal spot for large crowds; its neutral colors provide an ideal backdrop for red poinsettias. Gerry also uses white snowflakes and tiny white lights during her holiday decorating. Gerry refers to a goose carved by folk artist Craig Yenke as the 'Christmas Goose that never gets cooked'.

Chapter 2

Mark Kimball Moulton and Lane Carpenter

Mark Kimball Moulton and Lane Carpenter have done it again!! They have taken a run-of-the-mill house and renovated it to a work of art! I've followed Mark and Lane, figuratively speaking, through the various homes they have inhabited over the past 20 years and in fact have featured three of their homes in previous books as well as their gardens. While some of us apply a fresh coat of paint, or move a few pieces of furniture around, Mark and Lane thrive on just 'moving'!

This home is named Sparrowood and is located in the center of Avon, Connecticut. Contrary to previous homes they have owned , located on rural back roads, Mark and Lane are enjoying the proximity to the center of a village and all the amenities that affords.

Some of you may recognize Mark's name from the numerous children's books he has written.

Mark and Lane's house was built in the early 19thC and is painted with a Cabot solid stain called 'Barn Red'. Don't you expect to see Santa and his sleigh flying through the sky above the roof in the first picture?

The interior walls are painted with a Benjamin Moore paint "Taupe". A decorative architectural piece has been added over the transom window above the couch in the living room creating an impressive silhouette against the lighted backdrop.

The scrub top table is an early piece from Canada.

Mark and Lane created a Great Room by pushing out the back of the kitchen and building a large addition with floor to ceiling windows. The flooring is done with new pine planks which Mark has aged by laboriously rubbing black latex paint on each one then wiping off the excess before staining with Early American stain and polyurethane; a process which helped to darken the natural grooves and nail holes in the boards. The beams were salvaged from a 1700's house which was being razed. Everything seems to glow in the room with such charm and warmth.

Lane and Mark are the masters at reclamation and take great pride in the fact that they use salvaged materials whenever possible. The boards seen behind the step back cupboard came from the flooring of an 18thC home in an adjacent town. Mark and Lane stripped the boards and dry scraped remnants of paint to achieve the look they wanted.

The refurbishing of the house did allow the use of materials to address the comforts of living such as increased insulation but all the other materials throughout are reclaimed doors, windows and salvaged hardware.

Mark and Lane filled an early dough bowl with pomander balls they save from year to year. Another smaller bowl is filled with whole cloves. They leave the smaller bowl out with fresh oranges when entertaining so guests can make their own pomander balls if they choose.

A wax belsnickle and three trees of wax sit on the shelf in front of an early red ware plate.

I thought the idea of stringing the garland of lights on the headboard created a festive look.

Mark and Lane used more salvaged wood to give the kitchen pantry a rustic look.

Covers of some of Mark's books are shown to the right. They are sold through Amazon, Barnes & Noble and Mark's website at www.MarkKimballMoulton.com where a signed copy may be purchased.

Chapter 3

Chris and Sandra Foote

Despite a mild winter with little snow last year, a brief storm left just enough snow cover to create a holiday card-like scene of Chris and Sandra Foote's home.

Chris, an employee of Wegmans Foods, and Sandra, who works part time in the Human Resource Center at the University of Rochester, live in Hilton, New York with their two children Hannah, 10 and Collin, 6. Chris and Sandra's gardens were featured in my garden book, *Through the Garden Gate*.

Sixteen years ago, when Chris and Sandra were looking for a home in the Rochester suburbs, they were dismayed by the number of houses that had been stripped of all features of an older home. When they found their home, built in 1856, they were thrilled that it retained some of the charm of an early farmhouse. Their home features all its original moldings and, in fact, the extension at the back seen in the first picture was the original woodshed with a dirt floor accessible from the main house; it became known as 'the pit' until Chris and Sandy renovated the room and expanded the kitchen area at the back of the house.

Sandy used Sherwin-Williams "Rookwood Red" on the exterior trim, as it was one of the few paints she found that offered the depth of red she wanted. Chris received a call one day from a friend who had decided to get rid of a sleigh stored in his garage. The friend thought that Sandy might like it and would sell it for $100. Chris, not knowing if that was a good price or not but sure Sandy would indeed want the sleigh, came home and asked her if $100 was a good price. Needless to say, we know what Sandy said.

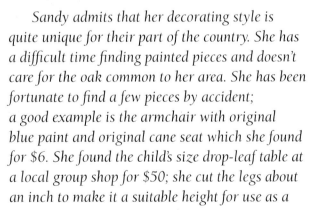

Sandy admits that her decorating style is quite unique for their part of the country. She has a difficult time finding painted pieces and doesn't care for the oak common to her area. She has been fortunate to find a few pieces by accident; a good example is the armchair with original blue paint and original cane seat which she found for $6. She found the child's size drop-leaf table at a local group shop for $50; she cut the legs about an inch to make it a suitable height for use as a coffee table. Because painted pieces are scarce, Sandy relies on reproduction painted pieces for color.

At the end of the sofa, an early single-drawer cherry table holds a new lamp fashioned with a reproduction lantern.

Chris made the barn wood bench between the windows; her Dad built the wall cabinet above it. Each year, Sandra's dad makes her a piece of furniture which she then paints and ages. Sandra painted this cabinet red and then applied a crackled black finish. Sandra found the fruit spray and large-handled basket at Good Old Days in Pultneyville, New York: (www.goodolddayscountryshop.com).

Sandy displays some of her Beaumont Santa collection tucked in the corner on top of the glass front cabinet; the Santas were gifted to her over the years by her family.

The kitchen eating area is located in the spot where the original woodshed stood. Chris created a frame for the floor using barn beams and then covered it with plywood prior to erecting the walls. The table is a married piece with a two-board pine top, formerly used as a cutting board to filet fish.

Sandy used Old Village "Steeple White" on the top half of the walls and Old Village "Valley Forge Mustard" on the bottom. The trim is "Plantation Red" also by Old Village, which Sandy also used on the dining room trim. Her dad built the surround for the electric fireplace. Sandy painted the landscape above the mantel.

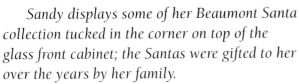

Sandy used the idea for making large gingerbread men from the book "Simple Greens – Simply Country". Instead of using dough, Sandy used brown wax and tied cheesecloth scarves around the necks.

Sandy's dad made the open corner cupboard; Sandy has filled it with handmade redware from The Genesee Country Museum in nearby Mumford, New York.

The tall slender tree in the kitchen is trimmed with small applesauce and cinnamon ornaments which Sandy and her daughter make each year.

Sandy collects pewter wherever she can find it. Seen on the large cupboard which Sandy's dad made, she mixes old and new pewter pieces.

A Belsnickel made of black wax holds a miniature wreath during the holiday season.

Sandy found the hired man's bed at a show over 20 years ago; she was drawn to it because of its original mattress ticking. The woman who sold her the bed told Sandy it had been in her family for generations and dated to the Civil War. Chris is a Civil War re-enactor, which also lent meaning to the piece. Sandy covered the mattress with tea-stained muslin and converted the bed to a window seat in the dining room.

Sandy found the large trencher at Good Old Days.

Recipe for Faux Baked Goods

3/4 C shortening
3/4 C granulated sugar
1/2 C molasses
4 C flour
3/4 C water

Cream shortening and sugar, add molasses and blend. Add 1 C flour and 1/4 C water at a time. Knead the dough and shape into a ball and place in a bowl. Cover with a cloth and refrigerate 30 minutes. Spray baking pan or mold with Pam and bake at 350 ° F. until dough is hard. This varies depending on the size and type of pan. In any case, the dough should be hard.

Dip your finished piece in plain melted paraffin wax to help preserve your faux baked goods.

Sandy used the recipe above to create the baked goods displayed on her cutting board. The key to preserving them is the wax coating she applies after the muffins and tarts have baked. What is great about this recipe is that you can 'dress up' your baked goods anyway you choose to look like the real thing

The kitchen in the house most likely dates to the 1940's. Sandy decided to paint the oak cabinets and carry the same mustard and red colors from the other rooms. The open shelving to the left of the sink and then far right is one feature Sandy liked in the kitchen when she first looked at the house.

Sandy originally thought of replacing some of the closed cabinet doors with punched tin but found them cost prohibitive. Instead, she removed the cabinet doors, lined them up and painted the mural on the four panels.

Sandy has an extensive collection of Rowe pottery with the star pattern, some of which is seen to the right of the sink. A collection of Beaumont pottery in the blue spatter pattern fills the first few shelves, seen right. The small tree is decorated with handmade ornaments made by Sandy and Hannah. She used the recipe below to create more durable ornaments than ones made with cinnamon and applesauce.

Gingerbread Ornaments

1 3/4 C sugar	1/8 tsp. salt
3/4 C honey	1 1/2 tsp. ground ginger
1/4 C butter or margarine	1 tsp. cinnamon
1 Tbsp. grated lemon rind	1/4 tsp. ground nutmeg
1/3 C lemon juice	1/4 tsp. ground cloves
6 C unsifted flour	1 large egg, lightly beaten
1/4 C baking powder	1 egg yolk, lightly beaten

In 4-qt. Dutch oven combine sugar, honey, and butter. Bring to boil stirring until sugar dissolves. Remove from heat, stir in rind and lemon juice. Cool.

Combine flour, baking powder, salt, and spices. Stir 2 cups flour mixture, egg and yolk into sugar mixture. Gradually mix in remaining flour mixture. Shape into ball; knead on floured surface until smooth. (Dough will appear dry before kneading). Divide dough in half, roll about 1/4" thickness on floured surface. Cut out with 5" cutter, place on lightly-greased cookie sheet. Cut a hole on top using a straw if you plan to hang the cookies. Bake 15-18 minutes at 325° F. until golden. Cool. Edible but cookies are hard and meant to be used as decorations.

Sandy liked the batten board ceiling in the master bedroom and gave it a new coat of paint. The walls are glazed with a mixture of gold paint and a glazing material which Sandy sponged on the walls.

The coverlet is a Family Heirloom Weavers' brick and linen piece.

The blanket chest was made by Chris' dad as a gift to Sandy and Chris. The mid-19thC clock on top is a family clock which belonged to Chris' grandparents.

When Sandy and her family aren't camping, hiking, or boating, Sandy is a co-leader of her daughter's Girl Scout troop and also consigns crafts she and Chris make at a local shop called Country Junktion located in Caledonia, New York; Country Junktion maintains a Facebook page.

Chapter 4

✦

Rich and Melanie Lortie

Rich and Melanie Lortie built their saltbox colonial 13 years ago in Sutton, Massachusetts. The house is patterned after a similar home in Deerfield, Massachusetts, with just a minor modification from a double front door to a single one. The house is painted with a California Historic paint called "Otis Madeira", while the front door is painted with "Hickory Nut", also by California.

Melanie was walking through Brimfield one day and spotted the sign now hanging on the side entrance; she couldn't resist it. Their house number is #80 and the date on the Poor Richard's Tavern sign is 1780.

Rich always teases her saying, "We're going to be poor if you don't stop buying so many antiques!" She claims that Rich cries 'poor mouth' but in reality Melanie is the spendthrift.

Melanie used a paint called "Grass" from The Seraph in the living room.

Rich is a self-taught cabinetmaker who has made numerous pieces for their home; the pipe box to the left of the fireplace is one example. Melanie appreciates each piece Rich makes and marvels at his talent. Rich enjoys working with wood and never hesitates to take on another project, as he would rather have one of his pieces in their home than one made by someone else. Melanie bought the vintage shoes from Rick Fuller. The candlestand is one of the first antiques Melanie purchased. The demi-lune table to the right of the fireplace is another piece Rich made. Painting floor cloths is one of Melanie's many talents; the large floor cloth in the living room was a joint effort with Rich. Melanie admits she did not have the patience to measure and draw the large compass in the center and relied on Rich's engineering mind to draw the pattern.

Melanie sometimes places the early tavern table in the center of the room, but while I was there she wanted to allow a clear view of the patterned floor cloth.

Rich made the beautiful chest of drawers and has completed three banister back chairs to date. Rich favors the William and Mary period and particularly enjoys working on pieces with turnings.

Rich made both the desk and the small corner cupboard above it. Melanie completes the pieces by painting black over a red base with a dry brush. The small cupboard is filled with her late mother's figurine collection; each figurine holds a special meaning. Melanie keeps the collection behind a closed door during the year but opens the cupboard and brings out memories of her mother during the holidays.

I could have moved into this room! Each angle had something to gaze upon. The round hutch table dates to the late 1600's and was purchased from Doreen Taggart in Richmond, New Hampshire. A pineapple sits in a large beehive bowl in the center. Hanging from one chair is an early powder horn; a frontier sack purchased from a now closed shop in Douglas, Massachusetts, The Keeping Room, hangs from another.

The jelly cupboard in the corner was stored in Rich's father's basement and was beyond salvaging. Melanie worked her magic and created a surface that is difficult to distinguish from the real thing.

Melanie purchased the large firkin from Molly Garland Antiques.

Rich made the armchair in the corner and the wall box from old boards with aged patina. Melanie's twig tree is sparsely decorated with ornaments of neutral colors.

Melanie purchased the large corner cupboard from Ed and Karan Oberg of Richmond House Antiques in Ashford, Connecticut.

The early scrub top table with red base was purchased at Brimfield from Rick Fuller.

Melanie confesses to her addiction for tables and chairs! Here in the 'tavern room', a large hutch table fills one wall.

A wax Belsnickel, made by Marsh Homestead Country Antiques, provides a nice contrast with the subtle color of the pewter plates.

I love the simplicity of the two long stockings hanging from the mantel. The colors of the stockings work beautifully with the muted tones of the barrels and contrast with the "Chocolate Brown" paint by California.

A large beehive bowl sits on the center of the table in the Keeping Room. Rich insisted on the purchase of the musket over the fireplace.

Rich made the large cupboard in gray which Melanie uses as a pantry.

Melanie loves to paint. Her cupboards are painted with "Hickory Nut" . . . the day before they were red . . . and the day before that they were Seraph "Grass". After two days of painting she returned to the original color! Rich wasn't quite sure where he was having dinner each night but didn't care since Melanie was doing the painting.

Melanie keeps a cutting board over her sink and uses an unglazed redware bowl to replicate a vessel sink.

The small black cupboard was purchased from Mary Elliott Antiques.

Melanie uses homespun curtains to conceal her dishwasher and the stove.

Beautiful pieces of early treen are displayed on the counter and below the hunt board.

Melanie uses Bennington Tavern pottery for her everyday dishes. The earthy colors are perfect with the "Hickory Nut" paint.

Melanie had the builder create a small buttery off the kitchen where she displays an assortment of crocks and redware. A large peel with rich patina hangs at the entrance.

Melanie has filled an early grain bin drawer with Granny Smith apples. The small red table lacked a top when Melanie purchased it but she couldn't pass up its original paint. She uses an early cutting board as a table top but sometimes removes it and places a bowl in the center to display other items, creating a totally different look.

Three large unglazed redware crocks are displayed at the side of the enclosed refrigerator.

Melanie made the stenciled floor cloth in the sitting room at the back of the house. An early scrub top table serves as a coffee table and a convenient spot to watch television while having dinner.

Melanie purchased the wooden lantern below at *The Bowl Barn from Louise Villa. Melanie found the large cheese basket at a yard sale.*

An early barrel holds a small tree decorated with just a few red stockings and mittens. The box beside it holds a doll that Melanie gave to her mother one Christmas just two months before her mother passed away. Ironically, the small orphan doll carries a suitcase.

The large desk with original paint fits perfectly behind the sofa.

Melanie was visiting The Bowl Barn just as the large apothecary with original red wash was unloaded! It never made it into the shop.

I love the hanging shelf above it. Melanie had nowhere to place the small black chest she had purchased. She removed the lid and mounted the piece on the wall to repurpose it. As soon as I can find some wall space, I'm going to try it!

Rich built the stepback filled with greens, stick-legged sheep, and a basket of rag balls. Melanie has painted it numerous times depending on her décor in the room.

In addition to seldom putting a paint brush down, Melanie also makes all her own curtains and bedspreads. She often purchases her fabrics at Walker House in Brookfield, Massachusetts.

Chapter 5

Paul and Susan Benoit

After Paul and Susan Benoit's children left the nest and Dad and Mom no longer had sporting events to attend, they looked at each other and asked, "What now?" Using a map found in the *Country Register*, they began to travel and hunt. Paul works in IT for a local manufacturing company and Susan is the Director of Nurses at Holy Trinity Nursing and Rehabilitation Center in Worcester, Massachusetts. They are free, however, to travel and hunt on weekends. One of their favorite areas is Pennsylvania; often they find themselves heading out from their home in Sutton, Massachusetts, and more often than not end up somewhere in Pennsylvania.

The exterior of the Benoit's house is stained with a Storm stain called "Brown Cedar", while the trim is Sherwin-William's "Fiery Red"; the doors are done with a custom-mixed paint to match a mustard painted bowl that Susan carried to the paint store.

The main section of the house was built in 1977 while the addition, right, was completed in 1988 and creates a family room a few steps off the kitchen.

Susan purchased the 'sleigh table' years ago at a local Massachusetts store. The large Santa, shown right, was purchased at the now closed Family Creations in Pennsylvania

During one of their Pennsylvania trips, Susan and Paul discovered folk artist Tom Panetta. Tom is the creator of Krisnick – old-fashioned one-of-a-kind Santa figures shown on the mantel; each is individually sculpted with a clay paper and plaster compound and then 'dressed'.

A reproduction sideboard in black, a Christmas gift from Paul, holds a Partridge in a Pear Tree and a fabric Santa.

A small hanging cupboard with tin panels holds an assortment of small holiday decorations. The light on the table beneath was purchased at Family Creations in Pennsylvania.

Three wooden candles are displayed on the top shelf of the corner cupboard – another gift from Paul.

The tree in the corner is adorned with country ornaments and a small candle at the tip of each branch.

More of Tom Panetta's folk art Santa figures are displayed on the faux fireplace in the dining room. Susan has found she must call ahead and order the pieces, as they are in high demand.

The reproduction jelly cupboard was purchased in Sturbridge, Massachusetts and holds another Tom Panetta Santa laden with a chockfull stocking. The light on the cupboard was purchased at The Handmaiden in Sturbridge.

I love the simplicity of the decorated whisk broom hanging on the wall.

Jeff Dana, a local craftsman, redesigned Susan's kitchen and custom-built the cabinetry. The farm sink and counters are soapstone.

The small Santa on the counter was a gift to Susan and Paul from their son who brought it back from Germany.

Susan and Paul use the area off the kitchen as their everyday eating area. The table was made with old barn board flooring.

Susan's extensive collection of nutcrackers, which she started collecting when she and Tom first married, fills the shelves of the stepback.

Jeff Dana redesigned the master bedroom and built all the paneled doors. He taught Susan how to finish the pieces by applying black paint and then red milk paint. Susan covered the bed with a Family Heirloom Weaver's black and cream-colored coverlet.

The entire master bedroom is decorated in striking tones of red and black. Susan has tastefully placed small holiday pieces throughout the room.

Susan enjoys painting furniture and in fact has painted ladderback chairs for children in the family with their names, birth dates, and custom designs which she gives as gifts. She also paints boxes purchased in Pennsylvania and gives them as gifts to friends. When I asked if she had an example, she answered, "No, I don't have any. I give them all away."

Chapter 6

❧ ✿ ❧

Buford and Joyce Cook

Buford and Joyce Cook live in Canton, North Carolina in a house they built in 1974. The house sits on a mountaintop originally part of 150 acres owned by Joyce's father. Joyce has collected primitives since the early 1970's and remembers well how easy it was back then to find primitives. After listening to Joyce, I decided she offers new meaning to the expression, 'the thrill of the hunt', as she never hesitated to knock on doors or search randomly through attics and barns. Now she relies on three or four local shops and yard sales and enjoys the proximity to Asheville, NC which she frequents often.

When I asked what items she particularly likes to collect, Joyce wasn't able to readily answer, but as we 'traveled' through her house she said more than once, "Oh yes, I like to collect those, too!" You'll see what I mean!

One favorite of Joyce's is her collection of salt-glazed crocks and pottery. A wonderful display in the stepback is seen standing above a display of folded early coverlets, many from Delaware and all in red, Joyce's favorite color.

Joyce also likes vintage Christmas pieces of any kind. A small buttocks basket on the early pumpkin painted chest holds a few of her newer pieces.

Another vintage piece, a 'masked' Santa, so named because the face resembles a cloth mask, is one of four Joyce owns; it stands beside a small sled.

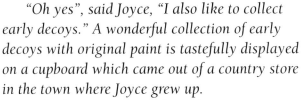

"Oh yes", said Joyce, "I also like to collect early decoys." A wonderful collection of early decoys with original paint is tastefully displayed on a cupboard which came out of a country store in the town where Joyce grew up.

Buford is semi-retired from the excavating business and is a Team Roper. He participates in competition as the 'Head Roper" and also has a leather shop on the property where he makes custom saddles and equestrian equipment. Buford and Joyce share a passion for horses, evident by the paintings and horse memorabilia scattered throughout the house.

Simple greens and pewter adorn the mantel of the large fieldstone fireplace. Built-in cupboards on either side are filled with vintage horse pull toys. Notice the early 'masked' Santa figures on the hearth along with the graduated stack of firkins.

The painting over the mantel serves as a reminder of the days when Joyce showed quarter horses, which she gave up "when antiques came along."

Joyce, a retired schoolteacher, admits that as the years pass she doesn't change things around as much as she once did and leans toward simplifying her home. She said there was a time when friends would ask each other, "I wonder what Joyce is doing today?" and their answer was always, "Probably changing her house around."

Joyce painted her kitchen cupboards with a custom Sherwin-Williams color.

The galvanized tin meal bin is a Tennessee piece. A large trencher is filled with butter molds while the top shelf holds two of the five coffee grinders Joyce owns.

A large seed bin from a country store provides enough space to display two children's cupboards.

Looks like Joyce likes to collect apothecaries also!

The children's cupboard on the right is a signed northern piece. The stick-legged sheep are German.

An enclosed sun porch is ideal to display a frosted tree filled with vintage cotton-batted ornaments.

Joyce occasionally finds cotton ornaments but reports that their prices have skyrocketed.

A stack of large leather-bound books is seen on a 19thC pine jelly cupboard that Joyce has owned for years.

Joyce fills the small mustard painted corner cupboard, found at a local antique street show, with her early bears. The chest of drawers on top of the bureau may have once been used as a jeweler's cabinet; it holds a miniature feather tree with three wax angel ornaments.

The bed in the master bedroom is a reproduction king-size bed with turned posts.

A cupboard in the corner is filled with red and white vintage quilts. Joyce loves Americana and has decorated the tree in the master bedroom with red, white, and blue ornaments and miniature flags.

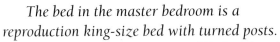

Joyce likes to decorate the screened porch off the back with more natural pieces, since it opens to the outside. A wonderful blue painted sled with paint decoration leans against an artificial tree with pinecones and white lights.

The three wooden Santa folk art pieces were made years ago by the late Glen Harbin, a Tennessee craftsman.

When Joyce is not decorating her house, she is decorating her church for the holiday season. She said when she acquires a new piece she 'upsets the apple cart' and changes things around until it feels right.

She feels fortunate that Buford goes along with anything she wants to do inside the house and he appreciates how she decorates their home. Joyce said she could bring in a new couch and it would be two weeks before Buford might comment that there's a new piece of furniture . . . "But that's a good thing", Joyce added.

Chapter 7

❖

J.J. and Jody Coffin

J.J. and Jody Coffin and I first crossed paths four years ago when I visited Rantoul, Illinois to photograph their gardens. In fact, their garden is featured on the cover of my first garden book, *Simply Country Gardens*. Jody and J.J. are each talented in their own right. Jody has an exceptional eye for decorating their 1900 home in a 19C style. Jody is also a professional with a camera in her hand. She has converted this talent into a business of creating annual calendars that she sells at shows and a website listed at the back of the chapter. J.J., a master craftsman who operates his own business, *Square Nail Construction*, is highly talented at remodeling and restoring homes. Some of his work is shown in the Coffin's backyard where J.J. built the cabin in the background. You'll see other examples of his work inside their home.

Jody uses the smaller cabin for a 'girl's night' once a year. They refer to themselves as the 'Cabin Crew' as they relax in the cabin enjoying hot cider and dessert with a few laughs!

Jody decorates primarily inside and out with simple greens and berries. What a great contrast against the weathered backdrop of the logs.

Jody purchased the house in 1974 and five years later knocked out the wall between the front porch and the living room to enlarge the interior living space. At that time, they built the large fireplace which they have since converted to gas for ease of use.

The flintlock over the fireplace once belonged to Jody's great uncle and was passed down to Jody by her mother. Jody's uncle had the provenance showing that the flintlock once belonged to Benjamin Franklin.

The area where the standing doughbox sits is the former enclosed porch. J.J. and Jody make and sell reproduction rush lights similar to one seen on the table, shown left.

In the foreground of the picture seen bottom right, an early harness maker's bench holds a rush light made by Kathy Nugent.

Jody used Olde Century "Old Ivory" paint on the walls in this room.

Jody and J.J. found the 19thC hutch table with original red paint at an auction in Illinois. Jody treasures the piece as it is not the kind of antique that is customarily offered at an auction in the area. The underside of the table creates a lovely backdrop for the vignette on the bench. Another of J.J. and Jody's talents is that of making replica rush lights with heavy wooden bases, which they sell. One of their creations is seen behind the foot warmer.

A corner cupboard, one of the earliest antiques Jody purchased, holds a collection of assorted treen ware and gourds.

The standing doughbox dates to the late 19thC and retains its original red paint on the base. The small tree is decorated with miniature gourds, although they resemble small pears at first glance.

The hammered iron piece is a skewer holder and creates an interesting shape against the side of the hanging cupboard.

J.J. made the small hanging cupboard which Jody has filled with small baskets.

An early stepback provides ideal display space for Jody's Greg Schooner redware.

Jody and J.J. undertook major renovations in 2006 which they refer to as the 'log job'. Using logs from a friend and some from a company specializing in barn wood, J.J. lined the interior walls of the dining room and kitchen to give the room the appearance of a log cabin. At that time, they removed the wall between the dining room and kitchen and logged the first floor bathroom which can be seen at the end of the room. The project took 13 months to complete.

The door at the end of the room leads to the bathroom which J.J. reconfigured and logged with leftover logs. The doors are early shutters from Pennsylvania and enclose the shower. J.J. poured the concrete sink.

A shelf above the shower holds a vignette of small log cabins.

A cozy eating area is located at the end of the working kitchen area.

The maple table is an old slaughtering table from Vermont. Jody decorates with gourds throughout the year; some are scattered around the floor. A yellowware bowl on the table holds redware and yellowware ornaments nestled in greens.

The large apothecary belonged to Jody's mother; it retains all the original porcelain knobs and has tin-lined drawers. A collection of belsnickels of varying sizes and colors stands on top.

The large candle, shown below, is encased with cinnamon sticks. Jody preserves it by using a small votive in the hollow core so the exterior remains intact year to year.

J.J. made the bed in the master bedroom using old Amish barn wood. Jody made the quilt on the bed. The trim paint in the bedroom is called "Trustee's Office Brown" and was found at Shaker Village in Pleasant Hill, Kentucky.

Jody and J.J.'s master bedroom measures almost 32' long which allows space for a sitting room at one end. Simple greens dress the mantel. Jody liked the color of the master bedroom so much that she painted the guest room and upstairs hallway trim the same color which sometimes looks green and other times has a tan hue.

A 19thC rope bed fills the corner in one of the guest rooms.

Jody can be found on picture trail at www. picturetrail.com/countryspirit. To order a calendar, Jody and J.J. may be reached by email at squarenailjjjc@mchsi.com or by phone at 217-892-4048.

Chapter 8

John and Linda Haney

In 2003, John and Linda Haney, both Illinois natives, purchased 80 acres in Coulterville, Illinois with the intention of developing the property; the acreage included a 12-acre lake. John and Linda were fortunate that they were able to sell the building lots almost immediately and began to clear their 10-acre portion in preparation for building the home they had always dreamed of. For years, Linda said she and John toured log homes and attended shows to research log home plans. They hired a company to erect the logs but Linda and John did all the chinking, flooring, electrical, plumbing, and the roof themselves. By 2009, working 24/7, they had completed and were able to move into the lower level of the log home consisting of a kitchen, family room, two bedrooms and bath while they worked on the main level. When I interviewed Linda, she and John were putting the finishing touches on the kitchen cabinets and hoped within the next month to move to the main floor after four years! John is a millwright and operates his own custom-built furniture business called *Bittersweet Ridge Woodworking*. Each piece that John creates is constructed with mortise and tendon joints for durability and appearance. Linda, until she devoted excess hours to the construction of their home, maintained an antique shop for 19 years called *Bittersweet Ridge Antiques*. Evidence of their backgrounds and talents is found throughout their home which is decorated in a style that Linda defines as 'colonial primitive'.

The expansive front porch provides space for Linda to display country pieces. The huge tobacco basket holds a wreath and early hurricane lantern. Linda has filled a vintage feed sack with red burlap-wrapped boards to represent gifts in the sack. The boards add weight against the wind and the green burlap ribbon provides more color.

Each window is dressed with a wreath and large red and white striped candy cane.

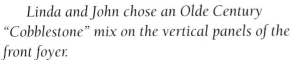

Linda and John chose an Olde Century "Cobblestone" mix on the vertical panels of the front foyer.

Linda's grandmother and her eight sisters created quilt tops for Quilts by Donna, which is still in existence. One of the quilts Linda's grandmother made is draped over the primitive settee in the foyer. Hanging above the settee, a framed appliqué of a barn and sheep was done by folk artist Bev Walters.

Bev Walters also created the snowman appliqué on the opposite wall.

An antique plantation desk is affixed to the wall across from the settee. Seen on the desk is a plat book, the property and land records of the county where John was born. The book dates to 1920 and records acreage owned by John's grandfather. Collections of bottle brush trees and small reproduction belsnickels are displayed on the top of the desk.

Linda hooked the rug which hangs above another holiday vignette in the foyer. Linda couldn't resist the unique black Santa created by Arnett's Country Store. The small child's red wool coat holds a vintage leather glove, a gift from John. A pair of vintage children's books sits beneath the small tree decorated with small red stockings.

Linda's father and grandfather were miners; their picture hangs above the small shelf containing pieces of spar, the mineral they mined in Kentucky. Linda's father carved the pieces of brilliantly colored spar resembling diamonds that Linda displays on the shelf. Linda explained that spar is used in paints and aluminum products. On the top shelf, Linda has placed her father's miners light worn on his hat. A wooden box stands on a piece of Kentucky 'redwork' fabric on the chest of drawers.

Down the hallway, a 19thC hanging cupboard with original red paint holds vintage books, a wax rabbit made by Marsh Homestead Antiques, and miniature ceramic animals.

John made the large secretary and finished the piece with an old paint surface; it features a slant front board which pulls out and up on the bottom to reveal the writing surface. Linda referred to John as her 'soul mate' and explained that she merely describes a piece and John is able to interpret her ideas and convert them into a design sketch.

The portrait over the mantel is an original, signed oil by Dutch artist Karl Rodweder Ruge. Linda chose the picture because of its tranquil depiction of a desk and early candle and its dark red paint that blended nicely with the room.

Linda grew up in a musical family. The violin resting on the hearth reminds her of the Kentucky bluegrass country music she was surrounded with as a child. Linda enhanced the vignette with rolled pieces of bluegrass sheet music and a large bow made from ribbon with pictures of violins.

The coffee table in front of the Johnston Benchwork's sofa holds a pewter tea set.

Tucked beneath the secretary, a nativity arranged in an early pig trough is comprised of ceramic pieces that Linda made, painted, and stained.

Linda hung a powder horn from the painting of George Washington at Valley Forge; John made the powder horn from a cow's horn. The quilt on the chair beneath it belonged to John's grandmother. A dome-lidded early document box is displayed on the hunt board, while beneath the sideboard three jugs including a redware jug by S&J Pottery are barely visible.

Linda made the folk art animals displayed on the early cupboard with original mustard paint.

I'm not sure I would ever leave this Keeping Room if I lived in this house! Linda grew up on the banks of the Ohio River in Pope County in southern Illinois. Her childhood memories are so strong of her life there as well as just across the river on her grandparent's Kentucky farm, that when it came time to build the three fireplaces in the cabin, Linda insisted the stone come from Pope County . . . and it is magnificent stone as you can see!

The sawbuck table in front of the primitive settle is an early piece and the perfect size for a coffee table. The braided rug beneath it is also vintage.

Linda decorated the mantel with a garland of faux popcorn and cranberries. The 30-day calendar clock hanging over the mantel was handed to her by her grandfather when she was 20 years old.

Linda has placed a vignette of antique toys beneath the Christmas tree. There is an accordion doll's bed with the original label dating to 1809, and two early excelsior stuffed dolls, one of which features a unique tin head.

The antique wagon under the window was found in Tennessee and was a gift one holiday from John. The large Santa on the mule is from Arnett's Country Store.

Linda trimmed the German 7' tree with slices of quince and berries. She found the cotton batting ornament at an antique shop but isn't certain whether it is an early piece or reproduction.

The plank top farm table is actually a biscuit table. A cutting board on the side pulls out making it ideal for baking and kneading dough. John and Linda's property is rich in nuts and pods, some of which Linda has used to fill an early treenware bowl.

John custom made all the kitchen cabinets; Linda selected Olde Century "Cobblestone" paint as the finish. Linda's countertops are poplar and were originally intended to be a temporary choice. Linda thought she wanted zinc countertops but is pleased with the poplar and has decided they are permanent.

In a hallway leading to the back kitchen door, Linda displays some of the aprons and bonnets she has made with vintage fabrics.

Linda filled a primitive pig trough in the corner with miniature ceramic pottery made by the Maple City Pottery Company.

An early wagon box in red paint holds a bottle and wax candle from Marsh Homestead Antiques.

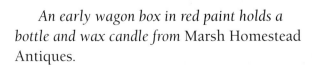

Linda decorated the stairwell leading to the lower level with an early wooden crate, a candle, and greens.

John hand planed each of the rustic mantels in the house. A vintage red and white quilt hangs on a blanket crane at one end on the fireplace in the master bedroom.

Although John and Linda's time for the past five years has been consumed with clearing and building their home, Linda manages to find time to create folk art fabric dolls and animals, sew bonnets, and enjoy her favorite pastime – decorating and redecorating their home. John also offers custom cabinetry. They maintain a website, www.picturetrail.com/bittersweetridge and can be reached at 618-318-1136.

Chapter 9

❦

Steve and Kathy Pastore

Steve and Kathy Pastore hope they landed at last in a home they will live in for a while. Steve, from the Philadelphia area, met Kathy when they both attended Villanova. They were married in 1986 and Steve, an engineer with a chemical company, was transferred to Houston where, as Kathy said, "They survived Katrina." They returned to Pennsylvania in 2007 and live in Coopersburg, a suburb in the Allentown area. Kathy is an RN and works part-time as a pre-natal nurse educator at a women's shelter in Norristown, Pennsylvania.

Kathy had always wanted to live in an old farmhouse, but Steve wasn't ready to face the work and expense of an older home or 'money pit', as he calls it. As a compromise, they purchased a new house and Steve gave Kathy free rein to decorate as primitive as she would like. Kathy admits that in their conservative neighborhood where many houses are similar, theirs stands out as something different because of her country decorating.

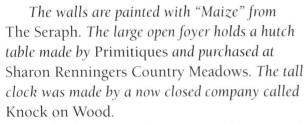

The walls are painted with "Maize" from The Seraph. *The large open foyer holds a hutch table made by* Primitiques *and purchased at Sharon Renningers Country Meadows. The tall clock was made by a now closed company called Knock on Wood.*

Kathy decorates with many reproductions and a few antiques. The sawbuck table was purchased at Aunt Daisy's in Emmaus, Pennsylvania.

Kathy purchased the cradle at Ginny Curry's Antiques in Ohio; it dates to the late 1700's and features a lovely cutout bonnet and original red wash.

The fabric Santa was made by Arnett's Country Store in Illinois.

Kathy shops at a number of stores and begins her holiday decorating the day after Thanksgiving. She and Steve host Thanksgiving dinner for 40 guests so Kathy does much of her holiday arranging and tree trimming in the attic, then carries the completed pieces down the day after Thanksgiving.

Kathy's trees are from Twin Feather Tree Company. The butterfly-shaped corner cupboard holds a variety of redware; many of the pieces were made by Greg Schooner and the late Lester Brieninger. Kathy purchased the Brieninger redware at a nearby shop, Country Capers. Some of the other pieces were purchased at Renningers Country Meadows.

Kathy painted the ceiling to match the trim, a Benjamin Moore called "New London Burgundy".

Kathy and Steve bought the 9' table in Texas; it took four movers to get it in the house. The base is oak and painted black. The black painted dining room chairs from The Seraph match the table beautifully.

I love the red stockings hanging on each seat and the candy cane striped candles on either side of the decorated centerpiece.

A narrow lift top chest made by Primitiques holds a Santa and lidded redware pieces.

Kathy painted the pencil post bed in the guestroom a matte black. The trim is Old Village "Valley Forge Mustard". The walls are done with Old Village "Town House Ivory". The glider horse, shown below right, was found in Pennsylvania, while the Santa was made by Arnett's Country Store.

Kathy used Family Heirloom Weaver linens on the bed and as a curtain over the faux fireplace, shown right.

Kathy and Steve found the toddler rope bed in early red paint at The Hen House in Macungie, Pennsylvania. Ginny Curry made the mattress.

Kathy has two handcrafted Noah's Arks in the master bedroom; the one below was made by a local artist from Lansdale. The 'Sunday Toy' Ark was made by Mo and Kelly Dallas, who Kathy met at a trade show.

Peggy Teisch hooked the magnificent rug behind the Ark.

The doll named Cordelia was fashioned by folk artist Judy Tasch.

Kathy and Steve's master bedroom had a sitting area which Kathy turned into a buttery. The primitive snowman on the table below was made by Arnett's.

Kathy placed a grapevine wreath on each window in this room which Kathy referred to as the 'other room'. The floor cloth was made by Jennifer Frantz.

Arnett's *made the snowman sitting in the chair in the far corner. Kathy decorated a pillow sham she found at* The Pottery Barn *with three knitted white mittens.*

Kathy has collected 15 game boards painted by Early American Life *artist Diane Allison.*

Kathy loves to decorate, do punch needle work, and cross stitch. Kathy loves primitives and doesn't mind a bit when her house is referred to as 'the museum' or her primitives referred to as 'part of the family tree'.

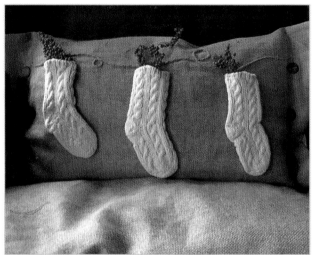

Chapter 10

❦ ◆ ❧

Ken and Betsy Heck

Betsy Heck is a Midwest transplant from Pennsylvania and met her husband Ken while they attended the University of Missouri. They built their home in Eureka, Missouri 20 years ago and have the good fortune to live close to antiquing in nearby Kentucky and Nashville; they also antique when they travel back to Pennsylvania to visit family. Betsy has developed a strong network of friends who share her passion for primitives and has found Pinterest a great source for friendships and networking.

Betsy works in the advertising/marketing field but as a part-time antiques dealer manages to find time for the antique hunt. She admits sheepishly that as she grew up in a home decorated in a traditional early American style, she swore she would never decorate that way; she planned on decorating with lots of glass and black leather when she got married.

But while in college Betsy developed a strong interest in history and began to appreciate the beauty of old pieces – their function as well as their form – and the worn patina of original finishes.

Christmas is Betsy's favorite time of year to decorate, and she has collected vintage Christmas since 1984. On the day after Thanksgiving, when most people are holiday shopping for Black Friday specials, Betsy begins her tradition of holiday decorating, and takes nearly two weeks to put it all together.

An early mule chest with salmon paint rests inside the front door in the foyer.

An oil on canvas depicting a pastoral scene hangs above a small wall cabinet that Betsy has filled with a vintage nativity, bottle brush trees, and German Putz animals.

Betsy admits to a weakness for yellowware and has filled the large stepback across from the front door. The 19thC blue painted box on top perfectly matches the blue bands of the yellowware.

Betsy purchased the large 19thC corner cupboard in robin's egg blue from Linda Rosen Antiques in Massachusetts.

The large lift-top desk in the corner sits on a separate base. The red wash is original; the inside of the desk is filled with small cubbies while the base has two doors. The table in the center of the room is early and features a single-board top with sage green/gray paint. Both the desk and table were purchased in Missouri from friends and dealers JHP Quilts and Antiques.

The walls in the living room are painted with Eddie Bauer "Reed" paint. An early hatchel with red, black, and mustard paint decoration hangs in the corner.

A painting of a Santa was done by folk artist Steve Shelton of Missouri; his works are often mistaken for historic pieces.

Betsy bought the blue painted dry sink in Missouri from friend Joan Lucas of Joan Lucas Antiques (www.joanlucasantiques.com). Betsy had admired the piece in Joan's home for many years, and when Joan decided to sell it, Betsy jumped at the chance; it is one of her favorite pieces.

Betsy leaves the hanging cupboard filled with Santa candy containers, brush trees, and metal German deer open all year long.

A collection of vintage belsnickels can be seen beside a stack of early blue painted pantry boxes. Betsy was thrilled to recently add a rare black belsnickel to her collection.

Betsy refers to the small open blue hanging cupboard, another purchase from Joan Lucas, as the 'lighting' cupboard as it is filled with a variety of early lanterns, candlesticks, and Betty lamps. The small table beneath is a 19thC tavern table with red paint.

I love the lighting in the picture seen right. Betsy has filled this room with all of the best country colors. Talk about eye candy! Betsy and Ken painted the floor to look like a floor cloth. They used a record album cover to measure the squares and create the pattern.

I could look at this picture until the cows come home! The ladderback chairs are an assortment but each features red wash and an acorn finial. The penny rug on the table is a vintage piece found at Windle's Log Cabin Antiques in Pennsylvania. The large mustard grain painted cupboard was purchased from JHP Quilts and Antiques in Missouri. The small hanging corner cupboard with dry blue paint was purchased from Gary and Pam Voyles, owners of Country Treasures in Alton, Illinois. The wonderful farm table with blue legs came from Friends Together Antiques and the red jelly cupboard was purchased from Whitehorse Antiques, both in Rocheport, Missouri.

Betsy displays a vintage feather tree in each room of the house; this tree is filled with vintage Santa ornaments. What a wonderfully colorful stack of firkins!

The two-foot German Santa candy container was purchased at the Hermann Antiques Show *from friends and dealers Russ and Rhonda Blank of* Sparrow's Nest Antiques. *He stands on a vintage sled with a feather tree, lantern, and sheep pull-toy.*

In the kitchen, a large collection of white ironstone fills the old milk cupboard found in a local shop in the tiny town of Maeystown, Illinois during an outdoor antique show.

All the treen bowls feature old repairs, and Betsy has placed them so that the feather tree appears to grow out of the center.

When Betsy and Ken first built their home, they used standard oak kitchen cabinetry as they couldn't afford custom cupboards. Eventually, they removed the hanging cabinets and hung antique pieces and painted and distressed the bottom cupboards to age them.

Betsy's countertops are slate, her second choice, but they were unable to find zinc.

The mustard green tote on the counter came from Renningers in Pennsylvania; it is filled with old bread boards and mashers. The red butcher block at the end of the island was a true find from friend and dealer Joe Cardetti of Kracker Barrel Antiques in St. James, Missouri.

The salmon painted apothecary on the counter came from Barbara Hood's Country Store in West Grove, Pennsylvania – one of Betsy's favorite stops while visiting family in the area.

Apothecaries are among Betsy's favorite collections. This mustard piece was purchased in Greenwood, Missouri at an outdoor antiques show.

The master bedroom is decorated in tones of blue and brown. A vintage quilt can be seen hanging on one wall; a vintage coverlet covers the bed. The six-board chest at the foot of the bed dates to the early 19thC.

The small corner jelly cupboard, another of Betsy's favorites, features lovely blue paint and honest signs of wear.

The early bench in front of the hearth holds a small feather tree, the first of Betsy's collection and an anniversary gift from Ken. Vintage stuffed bears share the bench. The doll in the make-do chair was made by Betsy's friend – antiques business partner and folk artist Dawn Alley.

Lisha Holt, co-owner of American Harvest Antiques in Paducah, Kentucky painted the door panel over the mantel. A collection of vintage and folk art Santa figures lines the fireplace mantel.

A folk art paper mache Santa was made by Missouri artist Elaine Taylor. The painting on the blue cupboard is by folk artist Anne Childs.

When Betsy isn't working, hunting for antiques, or cheering on the Missouri Tigers, she manages to find time to do a few antique shows each year and sell pieces out of her home by word of mouth. For the past 10 years she has partnered with Dawn Alley to manage Central Avenue Antiques. Betsy may be reached by email at centralavenue210@aol.com. They also sell antiques on Etsy.com.

Don't bother to email Betsy about the blue dry sink or small blue hanging cupboard in the dining room. I've already asked!

Chapter 11

❧ ✿ ☙

Ron and Sandi Cournoyer

Sandi's story is one of inspiration and a very happy ending!

Sandi and her husband Ron live in a home which resembles nothing like it did when Sandi, then a single mom, purchased it almost 20 years ago. Sandi at the time was employed as a hairdresser and worked two days a week. What was once her 'fun money' became the sole income for her and her six year old daughter, Lauren.

Sandi found the condemned house, built in 1952, in Sutton, Massachusetts. Sandi remembers wearing a mask because for almost five years, the house was inhabited solely by cats. The porch had fallen off and a dirt path led to what was once the front door. Sandi's brother taught her how to use a crowbar and hammer; while he helped her replace the flooring, Sandi single-handedly removed the tiles in the ceiling and the walls.

Sandi continued to work two days a week and each year identified another major project to tackle. Four years after moving in, Sandi met Ron.

Over the next few years Sandi and Ron accomplished major changes.

Ron together with Sandi's brother built the primitive cupboard that conceals a flat screen television.

An early child's sled sits atop the corner cupboard. Sandi has placed a small twig tree in a bail-handled pantry box on top of the stack in front of the window.

A graduated stack of 19thC barrels holds a small umbrella filled with greens.

Sandi used wallpaper to create a mural affect in the stairwell leading to the lower level.

A large black crow is perched on the end of a 'Massachusetts' sign, shown left. An hourglass stands on the back of a lift top desk scattered with replicas of vintage documents and newspapers.

A doorway leads to the back of the house and stairway leading to the family room downstairs. Early firkins and a large crock are displayed on a contemporary cupboard.

A vintage pair of snowshoes creates a holiday wall decoration at the top of the stairs.

A guest bathroom is located off the hallway. Sandi used an insert from an early trunk as a display shelf for her wooly stick-legged sheep.

Sandi uses one of the light switch boxes she purchased from Marsh Homestead Country Antiques to cover the tissue roll.

Sandi has filled her laundry room with utility type pieces. Sitting on the side of her washer was a huge glass jar of white powder which Sandi calls her 'Sandi's Suds', the very best detergent she has ever used. She says it far outlasts grocery store detergent at a fraction of the cost and was nice enough to share her special recipe:

In 2005, Ron and Sandi built a large addition on the back of the house which enlarged the kitchen and added a master bedroom and bath.

Sandi repurposed an early box and applied an old paint to finish it. A pair of mortar and pestles fit perfectly on the top shelf.

Sandi's Suds

1   4lb box of Arm & Hammer Baking Soda
1   4lb box of Borax
1   3lb box of Arm & Hammer Super Washing Soap
1   3lb box of Oxyclean
Grate 4 bars of Fels Naptha Soap
2 containers of Downey Unstoppables

Mix together in a trash bag and store in a glass tin or plastic container. Use two tablespoons per load.

Sandi found the primitive island at a local antique shop. Sandi modified two old boxes seen on the counter to the right of the stove; they now cover her coffee pot and microwave.

Sandi's countertops are tumbled marble tiles; she likes the color and the ease of maintenance.

A dough bowl filled with greens and fresh pineapple stands on an early child's sled.

The large open cupboard is filled with crocks, jugs, and scattered fresh greens and fruit.

Sandi used a collection of old measures to hang on the wall and has filled them with holiday accents and tin molds.

The curtain over the contemporary apothecary conceals a small television at the far end of the dining area.

The standing 19thC dough box was purchased from a friend. Sandi uses a large firkin with attic surface to fill the corner with a twig tree decorated with country ornaments and orange slices. A string of dried gourds hangs simply across the mantel. A large early basket sits in the contemporary settle.

When I photographed Sandi and Ron's house, their guestroom was arranged with the furniture seen below, while the master bedroom contained a contemporary cherry bedroom suite. I suggested Sandi reverse the furniture, which she did, and everyone is pleased with the result – even Ron – who had to do the heavy lifting.

Sandi used an old butter churn with chalky dry white paint to create a perfect side table.

As most of us would understand, as one thing is changed a domino effect takes place. The new bedroom was all it took for Sandi to plunge into the master bath and age it, a project she had wanted to tackle for months.

I love how Sandi changed a contemporary bathroom with a Jacuzzi into a primitive decorated room.

Notice the before and after pictures of the vanity!

Sandi was fearful of the first brushstroke on the cherry custom-built cabinetry, but once she started, there was no stopping her. I love the change!

Aren't the small handmade holiday soaps great? Sandi sells these in her shop and has them tastefully displayed in old wooden trays around the Jacuzzi.

Sandi's primary focus of her daughter's first 16 years was to be a mother and instill strong ethics. When Lauren turned 16 and was looking for a part-time job, Sandi bought a business and she and Lauren built a successful partnership with San Laurent Hair Artistry in Sutton. Typical of Sandi's zest for adventure, by the time I returned to photograph the revised master bedroom, she had decided to open a country shop in Sutton called Worn By Time, located in the same building as the salon on Route 146. Hours are Thursday and Friday 11-5 and Saturday 10-4. Sandi can be reached at 508-865-6454 or via email at sanron583@gmail.com.

Chapter 12

❖ ✿ ❖

Ron and Linda Glen

Ron and Linda Glen purchased their Northampton, Pennsylvania home in 1987 after deciding they wanted a more rural area than Staten Island, New York to raise their two daughters. The reader may recall seeing their gardens in *Just Country Gardens*. Linda works as an assistant buyer at wholesale trade shows with Affordable Interiors by Fay, while Ron is a regional vice-president for a facilities management company.

The front door is painted with Ralph Lauren "Cottage Hill". Linda creates her holiday decorating each year by adding something new. This year Linda added the burlap swags and garlands of greens to her second floor windows.

A morning dusting of snow created the perfect backdrop for two galvanized buckets and a wooden box of fruit.

Linda selected Olde Century "Linen White" for the foyer trim. The tavern sign was painted by folk artist Peter DiScala; it hangs above a 19thC tavern table. Linda shared that its three-plank top is so patched with square nails that an acquaintance asked, "Did you buy it that way?" The small lift top desk made by Primitiques holds a book and inkwell with two quills.

JT Skolas Co. of Hollis, Maine made the black candlebox which holds a primitive black angel purchased at CoCalico Creek in Lancaster, Pennsylvania. Linda said that she and her friend argued about who saw the angel first – fortunately CoCalico had two.

Laurie Bosi of Pine Hollow Primitives in Ohio made the tombstone angel seen on the large settle beside the small tree.

The primitive snowman hanging on the door is from Arnett's Country Store.

Ron and Linda replaced all the doors in the kitchen with custom-made farm doors to blend with the décor. A basket and tea-stained stockings hang on the door leading to the mud room and garage.

Linda used Old Village "Pearwood" in the mudroom.

When Ron and Linda purchased their tract house, the cabinets didn't fit with their decor, especially after they ripped up the linoleum and put down wide plank floors. Unable to find just what they wanted, they contacted a cabinetmaker in Reading, Pennsylvania, who built the lower cabinets with legs to create a free-standing appearance, then applied, cracked, and aged numerous layers of milk paint.

Linda loves her soapstone counters. A small mouse named 'Betsy' sits on the counter in the corner and leaves a message in the journal.

The hanging cupboard with a crock shelf on the side is also a custom-made piece.

Because Ron and Linda spent all their time in the family room, the formal living room was never used. Ron had always wanted a Tavern Room and intended to make one in the basement; since Ron and Linda would soon be empty-nesters they decided to convert the living room into a Tavern Room. Andy of Good Intent Farms in Pennsylvania made the bar. The sofa is from Johnston Benchworks. Linda used an old cutting board to cover the top of the open standing churn and repurposed the piece as an end table. The cupboard in the back corner is a Primitiques contemporary piece.

Kathy Graybill painted the round tavern sign.

Peter DiScala painted the Publick House sign. Linda found the green glass hand-blown goblets in Williamsburg, Virginia at the Jamestown Glass House.

An antique scrub top table stands in front of the window between the bar and French doors to the foyer. Linda has decorated it simply with two glass goblets, a bottle of wine, plate of apples, and a small tree.

The thermostat cover, below right, was made by Doug of Old Thyme Sales in Indiana. A small Belsnickel from Ragon House sits on top.

Linda has filled the pine stepback in the dining room with redware pieces, most of which came from David T Smith. An antique crock in the center of the bottom shelf holds hedge apples.

The European trencher is early; Linda has filled it with fresh greens and fruit. The small redware slip-decorated dish is a Turtle Creek piece. Linda used a bolster pillow cover from Family Heirloom Weavers to create a table runner! Great idea and it looks terrific.

The snowman on the reproduction jelly cupboard against the back wall was handmade using old wool. The crow perched on the hat adds the perfect country accent.

Linda has filled the small tree in the corner with miniature hooked rug ornaments purchased at a local shop; a fabric bird sits on top.

Ron's father removed the wall between the kitchen and family room to create open space. Linda used Olde Century "Old Ivory" on the trim. The chair and sofa are from Johnston Benchworks, while the coffee table is from Primitiques.

Linda loves her home and it's obvious she enjoys decorating. She is thankful that she was always able to be a 'stay at home mom' when her girls were growing up and attributes her passion for painting, moving furniture, and redecorating to those days when her schedule was planned around her family's. Linda also loves to garden, which is apparent from the beautiful gardens and landscapes she shared in Just Country Gardens.

Chapter 13

Don and Carol Smith

Don and Carol Smith haven't roamed far from where they grew up: from the house they owned for years on the center green in North Brookfield, Massachusetts to the 1860's farmhouse where they have lived for 25 years. Carol and Don moved to the farmhouse because they wanted a quieter area than the center of town offered. They were fortunate to find a home with enough land so their daughter could build nearby and a house large enough to accommodate an in-law apartment off the back.

Don works in the boiler room at a local corporation, but when home he is a jack-of-all-trades and seems to be continually building or renovating.

Carol has worked at *Spencer Furniture* in Spencer, Massachusetts for over 20 years and 10 years ago suggested they utilize a section of the store as a country shop. Now, Carol is the buyer and manager of the *Primitive Country Shop* within *Spencer Furniture*. Carol admits her house looks like the shop.

Carol and Don used Olde Century "Cobblestone" paint on the exterior. The doors are Olde Century "Savannah Red".

The trim paint in the kitchen is Olde Century "Tinderbox Brown". The archway signifies the original end of the house.

Carol and Don conduct an annual open house the last Sunday in November and first Saturday in December. They charge $5 admission which they contribute to Toys for Tots, a favorite charity of Carol and Don's, a former Marine. Many people attending the gathering recognize the house from when they took piano lessons as children from the previous owner.

Because Carol has access to a wide variety of newer pieces, most of the Smith's furniture is reproduction. Don made the shutters on the windows.

A 19thC dry sink seen left is one of the few antiques Don and Carol own; it came from a local home and has been plumbed to the outside well and features an operating pump.

Carol and Don's daughter, Kelly Valeri, made the wax apples seen in the dough bowl. Kelly is the owner of Smalltown Primitives and maintains a website www. smalltownprimitives.com where she sells handmade country items online.

Carol mixes Olde World Pewter newer pieces and some older pieces as well. The blue banded large yellowware bowls on top are old.

The sun streaming in the side window casts a lovely light on all of the pieces in the room. The tall standing cardboard Santa is from the former Kennedy Company.

Carol used the small hanging corner cupboard as the ideal space for her collection of old and new sheep.

Carol and Don had just removed a large cast iron stove at one end of the kitchen. Behind it was a mantel which Don fit to the space. A carpenter then built the cupboards which Carol didn't waste any time decorating.

Carol used a custom-blended Benjamin Moore paint for the trim in the galley kitchen space.

I think the row of mashers on the windowsill creates a lovely silhouette.

Kelly made the plum pudding which stands on the cutting board covering the stove top.

Carol painted the floor cloth on a piece of linoleum measuring 13' long. Carol used a table square to cover the microwave at the end of the counter.

Carol used Olde Century "Old Pewter" on the dining room trim and Olde Century "Linen White" on the walls.

Carol made the floor cloth in mustards, red, and black. Carol and Don's son-in-law Kevin built the hutch table at the end of the room as a gift. Kevin is a meat cutter at a large grocery store and Carol convinced him that if he could cut meat, he could cut wood.

Kevin also made the bucket bench which he and Kelly presented to Carol as a Christmas gift. Kelly made the shelf, also a gift.

The large open two-piece cupboard was made by PinePatchPrimitives.com. The top conceals an opening into the den on the other side of the wall.

A collection of black wax Belsnickels from Marsh Homestead Antiques is displayed with a variety of pewter pieces.

Don built the wall cupboard using old wood; it conceals a thermostat and telephone.

The den off the dining room measures only 6'X8' but Carol has managed to utilize every inch. The painting over the couch hides the opening to the dining room. Carol hooked the small 'welcome rug'.

Three of the walls in the room are painted with a Benjamin Moore historic color "Davenport Tan". The fourth wall is Olde Century "Barn Red" which Carol carried into the adjoining living room.

The Added Touch made the couch in the living room from an early bed.

The make-do chair seen below left is from The Seraph in Sturbridge, Massachusetts, while the chair seen far right is from The Angel House in Brookfield, Massachusetts.

Carol made the hooked rug over the piano as well as the one on the piano bench. A large trencher, purchased at The Bowl Barn in Douglas, Massachusetts, is filled with greens and berries on top.

Carol inherited the clock in the hallway; it was built by Carol's uncle for Carol's grandmother.

Carol found the small wall cupboard at a yard sale for $6. She removed the glass doors, painted, and distressed it.

A vintage suitcase once belonging to Don's uncle rests at the foot of the pencil post bed purchased at Spencer Furniture. Carol did the hooked rug above the bed.

Don found the wonderful 19thC cradle with red wash at the town dump and put it in the barn thinking Carol might sell it at her annual yard sale. He forgot to tell her about it for days and when he finally did, Carol couldn't believe her eyes!

Carol used Olde Century "Buttermilk" on the top half of the walls and Olde Century "Cobblestone" on the bottom.

Don and Carol's second bedroom is their granddaughter's room. Local artist Susan Dwyer painted the portrait of her.

The bed linens are from Family Heirloom Weavers.

The child's bed was a gift from Don and Carol's daughter, Kelly.

Carol painted the scenic mural which she copied from the small painting over the bureau.

The Primitive Country Shop, located in Spencer Furniture, is open Monday, Tuesday, Thursday, and Friday 10-8; Wednesday and Saturday 10-5, and Sunday 12-5; it is located at 6 Old Main Street (Route 9) in Spencer, Massachusetts.

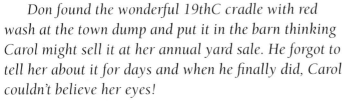

Chapter 14

⌒ ❋ ⌒

Mick and Sandy Deutsch

Mick and Sandy Deutsch live on 200 acres in rural Maple Park, Illinois. Mick farms corn and soy beans on 1400 acres while Sandy has an exciting career working for an auctioneer, being a 'picker' for a number of antique dealers, running estate sales and having yard sales. All of that means, Sandy often has the cream of the crop at these various sales and auctions. Their house is full of treasures that she has had the good fortune to accumulate through the years.

Mick comes from a family of grain farmers while Sandy is a dairy farmer's daughter. They met in their early teens through the FFA , Future Farmers of America, and dated through high school before going their separate ways. They reconnected and married twenty years ago and live in the farmhouse where Mick grew up.

As some of us can understand blending furnishings is not always an easy compromise. In fact Sandy had a difficult time with Mick's décor which was modern. She was strongly opposed to Mick's John Wayne light up pictures and popcorn ceilings. When the time came to move Sandy's belongings to the 'farmhouse' Mick was mortified that the truck passing through town, resembling a little like something out of Sanford & Sons, was headed for his place. The twig chair almost sent him running! Since that time though Sandy now says Mick has gotten into the adventure of it all and often comes home with things he's picked up in his travels.

The early baker's cabinet with tin bins stands on the front porch and was purchased for the fact that it blends perfectly with the pair of bowback Windsor chairs. Why you ask? Sandy found the pair of chairs at a yard sale and paid $5 each. They had seven layers of paint and it wasn't until she saw an identical pair on eBay® that sold for $1500 did she realize they were metal and thought best to hire a professional to complete the restoration project. The color of the metal blends nicely with the metal on the bins.

Sandy painted the entranceway of the 1917 farmhouse with a Benjamin Moore paint 'Brazilian Brown'. The pie safe with original sage green paint was a 'trade' for her services at an estate sale. They use the piece to hide their shoes when they come into the house! Sandy displays an early child's sled on top. Two of the three early paint buckets hold little lighted trees while the bucket in the middle holds pomegranates.

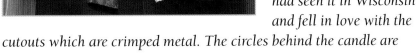

The hanging shelf above was a birthday present to Sandy from Mick. Sandy had seen it in Wisconsin and fell in love with the cutouts which are crimped metal. The circles behind the candle are copper reflectors.

An early rack holds mittens, a primitive sampler and an egg basket with naturals Sandy picked up on the property.

I love how Sandy has dressed three old boot jacks with holiday pieces. The boot jack on the bottom is unusual and was costly as it is made of one piece of bent wood in which Sandy displays a miniature holiday tree.

The living room is large enough to accommodate some oversized pieces. The 19thC chest in oxblood original red paint in front of the couch was purchased just short of a drag out fight. Sandy had first seen the chest at an estate sale and the woman selling the piece encouraged Sandy to come back and get it in a few weeks as the woman's husband was ill. The woman thought Sandy didn't want the piece and sold it to a consignment shop. Sandy called the shop and told the owner that she wanted the piece and was coming to pick it up but that it would take 45 minutes to get there. The shop owner called back and said someone was standing in front of her with cash and wanted the piece. Not willing to back down, Sandy told the shop owner in no uncertain terms 'NO' . . . SHE was taking the piece and her 45 minute was made in less than a half hour.

Mick replaced the popcorn ceilings with pine boards and added wide plank flooring. The furniture in the room is from Johnston-Benchworks.

A toolmaker's carrier holds some of Sandy's whisk broom collection and another small twig tree.

Someone brought the wonderful single drawer table to an estate sale. Sandy snapped it up faster than the blink of an eye! She was going to put it on the porch but decided it needed a place of honor in the living room instead. She bought the window above it at a garage sale for $100.

An early bucket holds a primitive Santa figure. The bucket stands on a metal door mat with heart pattern.

Sandy likes to display the measure standing on its side because the screen pattern on the bottom resembles the plaid pattern of her couch. The early spring holds a real bird's nest constructed around a clump of dryer lint Sandy had placed outside.

Sandy decided to decorate very simply this season. An early washtub purchased a few weeks before the holiday was perfect to hold the twig tree decorated sparsely with small candles and primitive ornaments.

The room is painted in a Pittsburg paint called 'Applesauce Cake'.

A 19thC child's sled in red rests on a jelly cupboard which Sandy found in a barn .Sandy made the 'Keeping Room' sign over the couch. She enjoys making them out of old barn wood. An early shelf holds as assortment of egg baskets, early lanterns, treen and a metal pair of skates.

The butcher block at the end of the couch came out of the general store in Mick's hometown and was a must have.

Sandy was shopping with her friend when she found the early store counter.

While she hated to pass it up, she had nowhere to put it in the house but put it on hold just in case. Her friend convinced her that Sandy didn't really need a dining room table as she had a large table in the kitchen. We know how that goes!

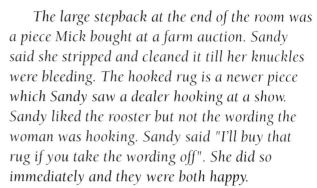

The large stepback at the end of the room was a piece Mick bought at a farm auction. Sandy said she stripped and cleaned it till her knuckles were bleeding. The hooked rug is a newer piece which Sandy saw a dealer hooking at a show. Sandy liked the rooster but not the wording the woman was hooking. Sandy said "I'll buy that rug if you take the wording off". She did so immediately and they were both happy.

Many of us attempt to replicate our décor to an earlier period which poses the problem often of what to do with the large flat screen television. Sandy and Mick conceal their TV with a barn door, shown left. They simply pull it across the TV.

A child's buggy seat in early black paint holds three pairs of child's shoes and a small bottle brush tree.

Sandy was thrilled to find the large scrub top table with oxblood base. She saw it at an antique show where it was marked $800. Each time she went around the show, that price of the table dropped in hundred dollar increments. They settled on $400 perhaps because the show was ending and there wasn't enough time for her to walk around another time.

A primitive Santa figure can be seen on the side wall beautifully displayed in an early strainer.

Sandy has placed a bottle brush tree on top of a graduated set of measures in the center of the table. Sandy wanted me to note the very unique Christmas tree cookie cutter standing to the right of the measures.

After Mick had remodeled the kitchen even he felt a modern stove would look out of place in the room. They found the reproduction one on the internet and had it shipped from Canada.

Isn't the make-do spoon holder on top fantastic? It's one of Sandy's favorite treasures.

When Sandy first moved into the farmhouse, there was a general store theme in the kitchen and the area above where the large buttery now stands used to consist of a wall of glass front refrigerators found in a butcher shop. Sandy found the buttery with layers of robins egg blue, no back and bright yellow on the backs of the shelves. After dry scraping it down to the green gray she was thrilled with the paint.

Each shelf is filled with eye-appealing collectibles. Sandy likes to have something small in the tiny drawers of spice cabinets. In this one to the left she has placed a pair of small graters.

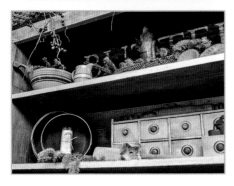

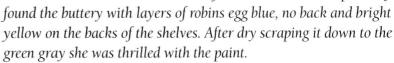

Sandy had just found the very large dough board which rests on top of the refrigerator which matches the stove. It was an anniversary present. The box to the right of the refrigerator hides the coffee maker.

Look at what Sandy came up with to use as a door handle? It's a hand grater.

An assortment of early advertising mirrors hangs above the stoneware vessel sink in the bathroom. The ladder holds an assortment of early coverlet remnants. Sandy placed the Santa figure in this room because it is made from coverlet remnants.

A small 19thC cupboard with original red wash holds a grouping of vintage bottles one of which reads 'Ligament Fit for Man or Beast'.

Every February Mick goes away on business for a week and never knows what he will find when he returns. The plan this year is to repaint the upstairs hallway and replace the modern railings with rustic stockyard fencing. Sandy uses an old farm chicken nester to display her salt glazed crocks.

A collection of signed and dated coverlets are draped over the railing which Sandy says shows off the coverlets nicely and, at the same time, hides the oak railing.

A table at the end of the hallway holds another small tree and an authentic abandoned bird nest.

Sandy managed to squeeze a primitive bucket bench on the top of the stairs and hide a belsnickle on the bottom shelf between two early crocks.

Look at the patina on this early farm scoop. It fills a large space over the stairwell. Sandy decorates it seasonally and has had great fun finding small pieces to put on it.

Vintage German sheep standing on the windowsill at the end of the hall look as though they are waiting for someone to arrive.

Sandy has done the master bed room in tans, creams and white tones. The walls are painted with Benjamin Moore paint "Grizzly Bear Brown'. Sandy found the beautiful cathedral windows at an antique shop nearby.

A leather bound book dated 1889 is open on the bureau.

Each crock or jug serves a purpose on the bed table. One holds the telephone and one the remote for the TV. The black and white picture is of Sandy's grandparents on their wedding day.

When Sandy couldn't find a bed she liked for the guestroom she decided to make it into a room where she could display favorite collections. Peg racks which used to hold her son's sport equipment now are used for child's chairs and baskets.

Sandy collects early lightning rods which represent a history of sorts for her. The pig is a reminder of the days when Mick used to raise pigs, the shortest one a dairy cow for her background and the steer in the middle came from her grandfather's farm.

Mick and Sandy have a number of outbuildings on their property which Sandy loves to decorate. When she isn't, the top right picture says it all!

Chapter 15

-►► ❄ ◄◄-

Mike Spangler

Mike Spangler has the house of his dreams – and perhaps that of many others of us as well! When still in high school, Mike happened upon a home in a neighboring town and then found the plans of a similar home in a magazine. He has held those plans in his head for a few decades. Two years ago, his Dad, a builder contractor, approached Mike and offered him a portion of the large parcel of land Mike's parents own. His Dad said 'Let's build that house you've always dreamed of!" Not only is the house exactly as Mike imagined, it holds special meaning as a result of all the memorable experiences of having built it with his father. The house, which took three years to build, is located in Charleston, West Virginia.

Mike stained the exterior with a Cabot stain called 'Barn Red'. After learning that the twelve over twelve windows he wanted were going to cost thousands of dollars, Mike researched online and found twenty-five sets of salvaged windows in excellent condition. They were in Brattleboro, VT, a mere thirteen hour drive away which didn't stop him. He pulled the seats out of his parent's van and drove the twenty-six hour round trip to buy the salvaged windows from an 1820's house for $20 each.

Mike and his dad made the door from a single piece of board milled at a local mill where Mike was able to obtain all the wood for the house from sub-flooring to beams.

Mike build the fence with left over pieces of rough cut wood from the sub-flooring of the house. The gate is of course old and was purchased from Connie Gleed. Mike is a talented folk artist as you'll see. You'll hear me say numerous times 'Mike made the . . .' throughout his chapter. In fact, the lantern hanging on the post is one of the pieces Mike makes.

Inside the front entrance, Mike placed a small twig tree decorated with tiny white lights and red and white striped ribbon resembling candy canes.

Although the folk art house sitting beneath the tree resembles Mike's house, he found it on line and had to have it. The primitive piece hanging on the wall is one half of a mold used to produce a machine part. The patina is rich which is what compelled Mike to buy it. Mike used Old Village 'Valley Forge Mustard' paint in the entrance.

An early leather harness with sleigh bells hangs on the back of the door.

Mike's twig tree in the living room is decorated with candy canes and white lights. It stands in an early work sled in front of the window.

The bears are perfect for the primitive armchair. The bear in front with its foot hanging over the edge is contemporary while the others are all early Steiff.

Here we go . . . the first of many! Mike made the large couch with a rope seat. He used pine and then distressed it. The trunk in front was a very special find for Mike. He purchased it at the Seville Antique Center in Ohio. Every nail on it is iron and hand hammered. Each side is a single board and it retains its original attic surface. The inside straps are original and go through the entire trunk from front to back. It purportedly dates to the mid 1700's. Resting on top, a small cricket cage sits beside an arm candleholder.

It was difficult to capture the vignette at the end of the room with the sunshine streaming in on the base of the scrub top table with blue paint. An early gameboard rests on top of the table. Mike made the two primitive candleholders, as well as, the shelves and signs behind the table. On the bottom shelf is a

folk art log cabin which Mike's Dad made when he was in shop class in junior high school. The horizontal wooden slats on the upper shelf are more parts of a sand mold most likely something with louvers. Again the patina made them irresistible.

Mike made the primitive high chair out of old wooden crates. The box above is one Mike designed and crafted also.

Mike's father had experience pouring concrete floors and then using a template and paint to create a brick floor. He convinced Mike that it was more economical to create this type of floor throughout the first floor and eliminate digging a deep foundation and pouring footings. Mike is thrilled with the result and reports that almost anyone who visits thinks they are authentic bricks.

Mike has five fireplace boxes in the house and decorates each one with exquisite taste. The insurance agent informed Mike that because of the rural location of the house, were he to build a center stack chimney to accommodate five working fireplaces, the cost would be prohibitive. Mike compromised and has the opportunity to decorate each without the cost and at the same time generated additional interior storage space in the house.

Mike used simple red striped burlap ribbon to decorate. The tin sconces were made by Carriage House Lighting and Tin in Ohio.

Mike made the wonderful high-backed settle with a rope seat and early feed sacks. He made it for the Simple Goods Show last fall and had many interested buyers but no one with room to get it home. Since the filming however, he has sold it. That doesn't mean if someone wants to order one, they can't.

A door from the living room leads to a buttery. Mike wasn't initially sure what he wanted to do with the space but awakened one morning a year ago, and decided he was ready to take the plunge. Just look!!

Behind a small mouse, Mike displays a cupcake tin which belonged to his grandmother. Dried gourds of varying shapes, sizes and colors fill the spaces around and between treenware.

Mike used the Seraph paint 'Earth' in the buttery and then applied wax to age the surface.

Mike made the primitive scrub brush with corn husks.

Mike and I both like looking at the picture on the left. The shadows of the window panes create a lovely look on the wall and dried gourds. The dry sink below is one Mike crafted from an old bench which had a salvageable top but rotted legs. The top of the bench is the side of the sink. Mike made the standing broom and garlands of lemons and dried green beans called 'leather britches'.

Standing back at the front entranceway and turning to the right, you enter the dining room. The tree in the window, dressed with small gourds and orange slices, stands in an old buggy seat resting on top of a chest.

Mike made the large farm table and wing chair at the end of it which he covered with feed sacks. An early carrier on the table is filled with greens and small dried gourds. Old and new redware is displayed on the hutch Mike and his Dad built. The third shelf down is lined with early tin-lidded Ball jars. The slatted chair beside it was a gift from his employer and was one of two benches which sat at the Old White Hotel, more commonly recognized today as The Greenbrier.

The desk was found at the Seville Antique Center. Hanging beside it is an onion lantern from The Seraph.

By now, I had the drift of it and knew before I heard the answer to my question that Mike had made the large settle bench.

Mike and his father built the large blue hutch before the walls were even up in the house. Mike knew he wanted to fashion the dining room around this piece. The contemporary redware creates a striking contrast to the color of the hutch.

The mantel is another indication of Mike's creative mind! Found in nearby Malden, the oldest town in West Virginia, Mike happened upon an old bed frame that was once used in one of the slave quarters at the salt mine in town. It was filthy dirty but Mike saw potential. After cleaning it up, the wonderful patina came though and Mike repurposed the foot board into the mantel in the dining room. It is dressed for the holidays with simple cranberry garlands and simple greens. Burlap ribbon hanging from the tin sconces add more texture.

Mike chose Old Village 'Salem Brick' red paint for the kitchen. The counter in the corner was crafted from a piece of wood left over from the front door. The curtain beneath the hanging cupboard hides the kitchen unmentionables i.e. toaster, blender etc!

Mike filled an early cobbler's carrier with greens, small candy canes and a candle. The island is of bead board construction with a poured concrete top.

Mike found an old wooden refrigerator shipping crate to use to conceal the refrigerator. A perfect fit!

Mike couldn't decide what to use for his island sink and vacillated between copper and porcelain. Then he spotted his grandmother's aluminum dishpan she had used for years to keep house. It was just what Mike was looking for!

'Waste not. Want not'. Mike used the headboard from that bed he found from the slave quarters to create the mantel front in the kitchen fireplace. How pretty it looks just adorned with simple greens and burlap.

Mike used Old Village 'Philadelphia Brownstone' a new paint in their product line.

Mike made the make-do chair and also the large hutch on the other wall.

Two treen plates sit on the scrub top table which Mike, surprisingly, didn't make!

Two belsnickels, made by Arnett's Country Store, rest on the end of the hutch.

Mike purchased the doll from Henhouse Primitives. Mike made the lollipop handled wallbox which hangs across from the door to the storage area under the stairwell.

Mike found the door in Ohio and when he reached home found it to be the perfect fit.

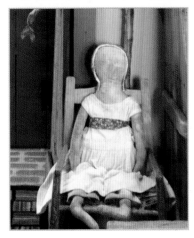

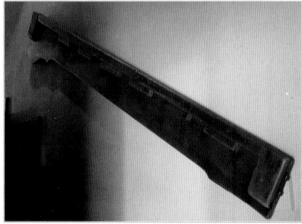

A contemporary feather tree is beautifully decorated with early ornaments, two of which belonged to Mike's grandparents. Two large Santas appear to be peeking around from the back of the tree. Mike was given the portrait above by friends and has named the sitter "Isabelle".

A tree decorated with red berry garlands, glass balls and a large burlap ribbon stands in the window of the guestroom.

I'll bet you thought Mike was done with that bed from the slave quarters! Nope! His father insisted on a railing for safety so Mike repurposed the last salvageable piece to create the railing with the bed side board. I was very impressed!

Mike made the bed which he finished in an early red milk paint.

When I first saw the Mammy's bench in black, I thought the back consisted of two silhouettes. Mike thought the same thing when he first found it at Creek Cabin Antiques in Teays Valley, West Virginia. Mike said it was missing the rockers and railing in front both of which he added.

A small holiday doll sits in a child's chair on the small hutch table Mike made. A sparsely decorated small feather tree with miniature candy canes stands at the end.

Mike purchased the small wallbox with original salmon paint from Alyce and Larry North whose home was featured in the earlier book, Autumn Harvest – Simply Country.

An old post office cupboard, which Mike has married with an early table, holds a collection of miniature holiday figures. The small nativity set on the top shelf belonged to Mike's grandparents.

The tree is decorated with popcorn garland and strips of red and white wool.

The Santa and two reindeer were part of Mike's family's holiday decorations.

Mike found the make-do table at the Simple Goods Show in Ohio. It is made out of an old Blue Label ketchup crate and is the perfect height for the tall bed in the master bedroom.

When Mike found the six board mustard chest at a local antique shop it was covered with layers of paint and decals. He caught a glimpse of what he thought was early paint underneath. And how right he was! Not only was the dry mustard paint intact, the back of the box was marked Mass 1732. It had two hidden compartments inside filled with old paper and a gold pair of early glasses which Mike displays on the shelf above.

Mike had always wanted a horse pull toy and decided to make his own with the set of wheels he had.

Mike used Lowes 'Burnt Cinnamon' paint in the master bath. Two vessel sinks rest on a marble stand which came out of an old hotel.

Mike maintains a website where he lists many of his marvelous primitive crafted items for sale. He may be reached through his website www.picturetrail.com/mikespanglerfolkart or directly at mikespanglerfolkart@gmail.com.